D1009195

Mornings *with* Fulton Sheen

120 Holy Hour Readings

COMPILED BY

BEVERLY CONEY HEIRICH

SERVANT
BOOKS

PUBLISHED BY ST. ANTHONY MESSENGER PRESS
CINCINNATI, OHIO

Special thanks to all those who cooperated in the publication of this book:

The Literary Estate of Fulton J. Sheen for permission to use excerpts taken from *Calvary and the Mass, Characters of the Passion, Footprints in a Darkened Forest, For God and Country, God Love You, Life Is Worth Living, The Rainbow of Sorrows, The Seven Virtues, Through the Year with Fulton Sheen,* and *Victory Over Vice.* Used by permission. All rights reserved.

Doubleday for permission to use selections from *Treasure in Clay* by Fulton J. Sheen. ©1980 by The Society for the Propagation of the Faith. Used by permission of Doubleday, a division of Random House, Inc. Used by permission. All rights reserved.

Liguori Publications for permission to use excerpts taken from *Lift Up Your Heart* (©1950), *Peace of Soul* (©1966), *From the Angel's Blackboard* (©1996) all by Fulton J. Sheen, Liguori Publications, Liguori, MO 63057, U.S.A. www.liguori.org.

Cover design: Left Coast Design, Portland, OR
Cover photograph: © Catholic News Service. Used by permission.

Library of Congress Cataloging-in-Publication Data

Sheen, Fulton J. (Fulton John), 1895-1979
Mornings with Fulton Sheen : 120 holy hour readings / compiled by Beverly Coney Heirich.
    p.   cm.
Includes bibliographical references.
ISBN 1-56955-040-9 (alk. paper)
1. Catholic Church—Prayer-books and devotions—English.   2. Lord's Supper—Reservation—Prayer-books and devotions—English.   3. Lord's Supper—Adoration—Prayer-books and devotions—English.
4. Holy Hour—Prayer-books and devotions—English.   5. Bible O.T. Proverbs—Devotional literature.
6. Meditation—Catholic Church.   I. Heirich, Beverly Coney.   II. Title.
BX2169.S497   1998
242'.2—dc21   97-45754
                                                                    CIP

ISBN 978-0-86716-842-6 (paperback)
ISBN 978-1-56955-040-3 (hardcover)

Published by Servant Books, an imprint of St. Anthony Messenger Press
28 W. Liberty St.
Cincinnati, OH 45202
www.AmericanCatholic.org

Printed in the United States of America

10 9 8 7 6 5 4 3 2

Acknowledgments

I am deeply grateful to Patricia Kossman, literary representative for the Estate of Fulton J. Sheen. Her devotion to the man she knew and continues to serve is a wellspring of grace and inspiration. "God love you, Patricia!" I'm also thankful to my Nashville writing partner, Jim Janosky, for keeping our fax machines smoking with daily prayer, advice, and encouragement; and to my business partner, Jennene Allen, for tremendous spiritual insights. Essential technical support was given with courtesy that blessed the work by David Scott Green, Gene Duran, Thomas Hedrich, Jarrod Psencik, and Terry Roby.

Blessings as well on the following for generously sharing their materials, prayers, and inspiration: Homer and Patt Hornor Allen, Susan Almadova, Claire Bawcom, Marge Bystedt, Jacqueline Costello, Jenene Dobos, Sharon Ehman, Liz Flory, Arthur Gordon, The Reverend Michael Hackbardt, Miriam Hellreich, Dr. Melba Kop, Helen McCarthy, Mary Anne Meyer, Linda O'Brien, Wm. Petersen, Father John Plough, Dr. Brenda Rambo-Igney, Dr. Harry Randles, Frank Ritter, Pat Robertson, Norva and Cheffy Skaggs, Caroline Boliek Wetzig, Dr. Jude Yablonsky, and my Jesuit professors at Seattle University who introduced me to the man who changed my life, Fulton J. Sheen. Finally, my forever-admiration and appreciation to Heidi Hess, a brilliant editor and a faithful prayer partner. *God love you, Heidi!*

Editor's Personal Note to Readers

This is not an ordinary book. In it, one of the twentieth century's most powerful and charismatic communicators passes on his secret about a simple, fail-proof way to become the better persons we sometimes dream we might have been—or may yet become. With his brilliant intellect, surprising candor, and winsome wit, Fulton Sheen has jump-started that dream into reality for millions around the world. He will do the same for you.

As you begin this book, you'll experience from the first day an incredible sense of having begun an amazing new adventure. Your reactions, even your own words, will begin to surprise you. You'll discover you have a new power over the difficult people and events in your life, perhaps including any disagreeable aspects of human nature you might possess. Best of all, long before 120 days have passed, you'll realize you're no longer identifying Christ with your interest in others; instead you're identifying yourself with His interest in them.

Who Is Fulton Sheen?

Fulton Sheen has been described as a man who changed more lives and brought more holy laughter into the world than anyone during the past hundred years.

This Catholic priest with piercing eyes was as popular a television star in the fifties as Milton Berle was, and as Jerry Seinfeld is today.

Every Sunday evening, with a small piece of chalk and a blackboard, he blended holy laughter and mysticism to introduce millions to the reality of an unseen world more real than any physical reality.

As his fame grew, he became one of the most popular personalities in the world. Television awarded him their highest honor—the Emmy—and he made the covers of *Time*, *Life*, and *Look* as "the greatest communicator of our time."

Even after he became a bishop, Fulton Sheen never gave the impression that he was too busy or too important to approach. His mail from people of every age and religious background set records. President Dwight D. Eisenhower was a fan. As a young actor, Martin Sheen was so impressed by the bishop that he asked to take Sheen's last name as his own—for life.

Once when Fulton Sheen asked viewers to send him a dime for the poor of the world, he was deluged with coins taped to letters. In his autobiography *Treasure in Clay* he wrote, "We opened a yellow envelope and $10,000 in cash fell out. Scrawled in pencil was a note: 'I don't need this anymore. God told me to give it to the poor.'

"Students sacrificed their high-school or college rings and sent the equivalent to missions. In one telecast I said I liked chocolate cookies. The following week we could hardly get in the door of the office, which was blocked with boxes of chocolate cookies."

Sheen began life as an ordinary and sometimes naughty farm boy from Peoria, Illinois. His family was well respected but not particularly illustrious. His father had a third-grade education. His mother went through eighth grade in a one-room schoolhouse.

What power transformed this simple man into one of the most beloved, brilliant, and influential personalities in the world? All his life, and even as he lay dying, Sheen insisted the secret to his power was grace that came through spending one Holy Hour every day in Christian meditation.

About This Book

Each page of this guide for your personal Holy Hour contains three important parts. The first section is a thought-provoking concept or personal recollection from the mind of Fulton Sheen.

Next you will find a congruent verse from the biblical Book of Proverbs. Why Proverbs? Harmonizing Fulton Sheen's spiritual insights with the life of action revealed in Proverbs integrates the supernatural with the natural. It is the Bible's book of practical ethics, written to teach us the difference between right and wrong, to help us succeed in life. Sometimes called the "granddaddy of every self-improvement book ever written," the commonsense advice in the Proverbs has never grown old-fashioned. As Napoleon once said, "If any man shall conquer this book, none but Christ shall conquer him!"

**Biblical scholars have said
other books of the Bible
tell us *what* to do;
Proverbs tells us *how!***

The third part of each reflection is a line that reads simply, "My Secret Meditation." This is a place to write your private Holy Hour thoughts. Be open before the Lord. What you write may be nothing more than a word or two, but if it comes from your secret heart—*where only your Lord has access*—it will be precious dialogue with Him.

At the end of 120 days, as you look back over what you've written, you'll be filled with wonder at how you've changed. Then you'll know these were not your original thoughts, but were given to you by the One Who knows you best and loves you most.

Your Guide to a Holy Hour

Are you intrigued by the idea of spending a Holy Hour with God, but unsure where to begin? Here are ten simple steps to help you.

1. Find a place where you can be undisturbed for one hour. It may be a church, a park, or a quiet room in your home.
2. Open this book as if you've lifted a telephone receiver to have a brief conversation with a wise friend, Fulton Sheen. Slowly and thoughtfully read one page.
3. Close the book.

4. Close your eyes.

5. Breathe deeply three times as you whisper His Name ... *Jesus.* He will be there.

6. With an act of your will, surrender completely to His Presence, and tell Him that you want to love Him more today than ever before.

7. When your mind wanders to personal problems or other distractions, bring it back to Him by whispering His Name. At first, you may whisper it over and over for the entire hour. This is a discipline to teach your will that here in this quiet place for this hour, self is not in charge. Jesus is Lord.

8. Do not leave before the hour has passed. At first it will seem too long. Soon it will seem too short.

9. When the hour is over, tell Him you love Him and will meet Him the next day at the same time and in the same place. Let Him know that He is your priority, and that you know He'll be waiting for you.

10. Before you go into the world, take a moment to jot down any thoughts and impressions that came to you during that hour. It is during these times of quiet reflection that the Holy Spirit can speak most eloquently to our hearts. Keep in mind that He works in the human personality at a very deep level, and that the deepest work is often at first invisible.

You Are Invited

"Meditation," observed Fulton Sheen in *Lift Up Your Heart*, "is a higher form of prayer than petition. It is a little like a daydream or a reverie; [except that] in meditation we do not think about the world or ourselves, but about God." *Watch with me one hour!,* Jesus invites you. When you say yes to Him, you begin the greatest adventure of your life. Your only task is self-discipline. The outcome is in the hands of God. He's waiting for you, longing to unlock mystic treasures hidden for so long from so many—longing to change your life in ways more wondrous than your dreams.

If you would like to become part of a worldwide Holy Hour Movement, to help make Fulton Sheen's lifelong dream come true, to encourage others to say yes to Jesus, perhaps to be in touch with them, and to hear how God is changing lives, we'll be happy to hear from you. Write to us, let us know what the Lord is doing in your life, and enclose a stamped, self-addressed envelope.

Meanwhile, never forget that you are loved and that every morning, Someone is waiting for you.

Beverly Coney Heirich

The following introduction is taken from Bishop Fulton J. Sheen's autobiography *Treasure in Clay,* written shortly before his death and published posthumously in 1980 by Doubleday. The publisher has graciously given permission to share it with all of us.

†

The Hour That Makes My Day

by Fulton J. Sheen

The Holy Hour had its origin in a practice I developed a year before I was ordained. The big chapel in St. Paul's Seminary would be locked at six o'clock. This particular evening during recreation, I walked up and down outside the closed chapel for almost an hour. The thought struck me—why not make a Holy Hour of adoration in the presence of the Blessed Sacrament?

The next day I began and the practice is now well over sixty years old. Briefly, here are some reasons I have kept up this practice, and why I have encouraged it in others:

First, the Holy Hour is not a devotion; it is a sharing in the work of redemption. Our blessed Lord used the words hour and day in two totally different connotations in the Gospel of John. The day belongs to God; the hour belongs to evil. Seven times in the Gospel of John, the word hour is used, and in each instance it refers to the demonic, and to the moments when Christ is no longer in the Father's Hands, but in the hands of men.

> **In the Garden, Our Lord contrasted two
> "hours"—one was the evil hour, "This is
> your hour"—with which Judas could turn
> out the lights of the world.
> In contrast, our Lord asked:
> "Could you not watch one hour with me?"**

In other words, He asked for an hour of reparation to combat the hour of evil; an hour of victimal union with the Cross to overcome the anti-love of sin.

Second, the only time our Lord asked the Apostles for anything was the night He went into His agony. But as often in the history of the church since that time, evil was awake, but the disciples were asleep. That is why there came out of His anguished and lonely Heart the sigh: "Could you not watch one hour with Me?" Not for an hour of activity did he plead, but for an hour of friendship.

The third reason I keep up the Holy Hour is to grow more and more into His likeness. As Paul puts it: "We are transfigured into His likeness, from splendor to splendor." We become like that which we gaze upon. Looking into a sunset, the face takes on a golden glow. Looking at the Eucharistic Lord for an hour transforms the heart in a mysterious way as the face of Moses was transformed after his companionship with God on the mountain.

**The purpose of the Holy Hour is
to encourage a deep personal encounter
with Christ.**

The holy and glorious God is constantly inviting us to come to Him, to hold converse with Him, to ask for such things as we need, and to experience what a blessing there is in fellowship with Him.

Sensitive love or human love declines with time, but divine love does not. The first is concerned with the body which becomes less and less responsive to stimulation, but in the order of grace, the responsiveness of the divine to tiny, human acts of love intensifies.

Neither theological knowledge nor social action alone is enough to keep us in love with Christ unless both are preceded by a personal encounter with Him.

**It is impossible for me to explain how
helpful the Holy Hour has been. Quite
apart from its positive spiritual benefits,
it has kept my feet from wandering too far.**

The Hour became a teacher, for although before we love anyone we must have a knowledge of that person, nevertheless, *after* we know, it is love that increases knowledge. Theological insights are gained not only from between two covers of a book, but from two bent knees before an altar. The Holy Hour becomes like an oxygen tank to revive the breath of the Holy Spirit in the midst of the foul and fetid atmosphere of the world.

Finally, making a Holy Hour every day constituted for me one area of life in which I could preach what I practiced. I very seldom in my life preached fasting in a rigorous kind of way, for I always found fasting extremely difficult. But I could ask others to make the Hour, because I made it.

Sometimes I wish that I had kept a record of the thousands of letters I have received from priests and laity telling me how they have taken up the practice of the Holy Hour.

A monsignor who was told to leave his parish because of his weakness for alcohol and consequent scandal, went into another diocese on a trial basis, where he made my retreat. Responding to the grace of the Lord, he gave up alcohol, was restored to effectiveness in his priesthood, made the Holy Hour every day, and died in the Presence of the Blessed Sacrament.

As an indication of the very wide effect of the Holy Hour, I once received a letter from a priest in England who told me: "I left the priesthood and fell into a state of degradation."

A priest friend invited him to hear a tape on the Holy Hour from a retreat I had given. Responsive to grace, he was restored again to the priesthood and entrusted with the care of a parish. Divine Mercy wrought a change in him.

Many of the laity who have read my books and heard my tapes are also making the Holy Hour. A state trooper wrote that he had my tapes attached to his motorcycle and would listen to them as he was cruising the highways: "Imagine," he wrote, "the bewilderment of a speeder being stopped by me while from the tape recorder was coming one of your sermons about the Eucharist."

The trooper found it difficult at first to find a church that was open during the day at a time he could make his Hour. Later on, he found a pastor who was not only willing to open the church, but even willing to make the Hour with him.

Most remarkable of all was the effect the preaching of the Holy Hour had on non-Catholic ministers. I preached three retreats to Protestant ministers—on two occasions to over three hundred in South Carolina and in Florida, and on another occasion to a smaller group at Princeton University.

**I asked them to make a continuous
Holy Hour of prayer in order to
combat the forces of evil
in the world,
because that is what our Lord asked for
the night of His Agony.**

One year later, a very distinguished Christian gentleman wrote and told me that seven hundred ministers had pledged one hour a day. About six years later, he sent this message: "We have now mobilized and trained over 100,000 One-Hour-Watchers."

I know thousands of priests who have not had the practice of making frequent visits to the Blessed Sacrament, but I am absolutely certain that in the sight of God, they are a thousand times more worthy than I.

In any case, this is the story of the means I chose in my priesthood to be able just to keep step with my brother priests in the service of the Lord.

Today, even this autobiography is being written in His Presence, that He might inspire others—when I am gone—to make the Hour that makes Life.

 1

Fresh Starts

Though time is too precious to waste, it must never be thought that what was lost is irretrievable. Once the Divine is introduced, then comes the opportunity to make up for losses. God is the God of the second chance.... Being born again means that all that went before is not held against us.

Peace of Soul

If you want to be a failure, never admit you were wrong.
But if you confess your mistakes and forsake them,
you get another chance!
PROVERBS 28:13

My Secret Meditation

_____

_____

_____

When God Is Silent

For meditation the ear of the soul is more important than the tongue: St. Paul tells us that faith comes from listening. (Most people make the same mistake with God that they do with their friends: they do all the talking.) God has things to tell us which will enlighten us—we must wait for Him to speak. No one would rush into a physician's office, rattle off all the symptoms, and then dash away without waiting for a diagnosis. It is every bit as stupid to ring God's doorbell and then run away. The Lord hears us more readily than we suspect; it is our listening to Him that needs to be improved.

Lift Up Your Heart

If we turn a deaf ear to God,
He turns a deaf ear to us.
PROVERBS 28:9

My Secret Meditation

3

The Two Loneliest Places in the World

The search for peace within the self is always doomed to fail; the two loneliest places in the world are a strange city and one's own ego. When a man is alone with his thoughts, in false independence of the Love Who made him, he keeps bad company. No amount of psychoanalysis can heal the uneasiness that results, for its basis is metaphysical, its source the tension between the finite and infinite.

Lift Up Your Heart

Do you want to understand why you do the things you do?
Knowing and fearing God results in
every other kind of understanding.
PROVERBS 9:10

My Secret Meditation

_____

_____

_____

4

Fear of People

Goliath was a great giant clothed in an armor of steel and carrying in his hand a mighty sword. David was the shepherd boy without defensive steel, carrying no other weapon than a staff and five little stones from a nearby brook. Goliath scorned him, saying: "Am I a dog, that thou comest to me with a staff?" David answered humbly, not trusting in his own power: "I come to thee in the name of the Lord...." The outcome we know. The boy with a stone killed the giant with the armor and sword.

"The foolish things of the world hath God chosen, that he may confound the wise; and the weak things of the world hath God chosen that he may confound the strong" (1 Cor 1:27).

God Love You

*If only our fear of Heaven
would be as great as our fear of man!*
PROVERBS 29:25

My Secret Meditation

_____

_____

_____

5

Bad? Who Says So?

What makes a thing bad? Well, here is a pencil. This is a good pencil because it does what it was made to do. It writes. Is it a good can opener? It certainly is not!

Suppose I use the pencil as a can opener. What happens? First of all, I do not open the can. Second, I destroy the pencil.

Now if I decide to do certain things with my body which I ought not to do, I do not attain the purpose for which I was created. For example, becoming an alcoholic does not make me happy. I destroy myself just as I destroyed the pencil in using it to open a can.

When I disobey God, I do not make myself very happy on the inside, and I certainly destroy any peace of soul that I ought to have.

Through the Year with Fulton Sheen

God blesses those who obey Him;
trust Him for happiness.
Proverbs 16:20

My Secret Meditation

_____

_____

_____

6

God, the Night Watchman

After a succession of hot, sultry days in the summer, we sense there must be a storm before the cool days come back again.

Similarly, in these days of confusion, there is an intuition of impending catastrophe, a feeling that some immense preternatural disturbance must bring the evil of the world to ruins before we can be set free again.

As DeGoncourt told Berthelot, who had boasted of the future destructiveness of war through physics: "When that day comes, God as a night-watchman will come down from Heaven, rattling His keys, saying, 'Gentlemen! It is closing time!'"

Peace of Soul

Justice is a joy to the innocent;
but Truth torments the guilty.
PROVERBS 21:15

My Secret Meditation

_____

_____

_____

Gold Rings

How changed the world would be if we worked as hard at being good as we work at making ourselves comfortable or beautiful!

God Love You

Like a golden ring in the snout of a pig,
is a beautiful woman without refinement.
PROVERBS 11:22

My Secret Meditation

_____

_____

_____

 **8**

A Cure for Depression

D epression comes not from having faults but from the refusal to face them. There are tens of thousands of persons today suffering from fears which in reality are nothing but the effects of hidden sin. The examination of conscience will cure us of self-deception. It will also cure us of depression.

Peace of Soul

The wicked run scared when no one is chasing them!
But the good are as bold as young lions.
PROVERBS 28:1

My Secret Meditation

_____

_____

_____

A Little Corner of My Heart

Every person has a little corner in his heart he never wants anyone to venture into, even with a candle. That is why we deceive ourselves and why our neighbors know us better than we know ourselves.

Peace of Soul

We can justify everything we do,
but the Lord sees our motives.
PROVERBS 21:2

My Secret Meditation

_____

_____

_____

No Time for Meditation?

I t is never true that we have no time to meditate; the less one
thinks of God, the less time there will always be for Him. The
time one has for anything depends on how much we value it.
Thinking determines the uses of time; time does not rule over thinking. The problem of spirituality is never, then, a question of time; it is
a problem of thought. For it does not require much time to make us
saints; it requires only much love.

God Love You

If we want to be wise, the choice is our own.
It's a matter of the will.
PROVERBS 9:12

My Secret Meditation

_____

_____

_____

Getting Dressed for Heaven

We cannot love sin during life and begin to love virtue at death. The joys of heaven are the continuance of the Christ-like joys of earth. We do not develop a new set of loves with our last breath. We shall reap in eternity only what we sowed on earth.

Then let not our presuming moderns who pile sin on sin think that they can insult God until their lease on life has run out and then expect an eternal lease on one of the Father's mansions. Did He who went to Heaven by a Cross intend that you should go there by sinning?

The Seven Virtues

Turning away from me is dangerous.
Your foolish self-confidence will destroy you!
PROVERBS 1:32

My Secret Meditation

_____

_____

_____

Television Talk Shows and Tabloids

A few decades ago, nobody believed in the confession of sins except the Church. Today everyone believes in confession—with this difference: some believe in confessing their own sins; others believe in confessing other people's sins.

The popularity of psychoanalysis has nearly convinced everyone of the necessity of some kind of confession for peace of mind. This is another instance of how the world, which threw Christian truths into the wastebasket in the nineteenth century, is pulling them out in isolated secularized form in the twentieth century, meanwhile deluding itself into believing that it has made a great discovery. The world found it could not get along without some release for its inner unhappiness. Once it had rejected confession and denied both God and guilt, it had to find a substitute.

Footprints in a Darkened Forest

Tell your secrets to a gossip
if you want them broadcast to the world.
PROVERBS 20:19

My Secret Meditation

_____

_____

_____

When You Are Disgusted

If you are disgusted with yourself, remember that you can come to God even by a succession of disgusts. That is one of the ways God makes you feel hunger for the Divine. Do you not crave food most when you are hungry? Do you not want water most when you are thirsty? Your own disgust, if you knew it, is the distant call of Divine Mercy.

Only when God ceases to be infinitely merciful and only when you begin to be infinitely evil, will there be reason for despair; and that will be *never!*

The Seven Virtues

Don't give up when God shows your failure to you;
it proves He loves you.
Just as a parent punishes a child out of love,
the Lord corrects us to make us better!
PROVERBS 3:11–12

My Secret Meditation

_____

_____

_____

 14

Virtue in Children

Why is it that the world has confessed its inability to inculcate virtue in the young? Very simply because it has not corelated morality to any love nobler than self-love. Things fulfill their proper role only when integrated into a larger whole.

Most lives are like doors without hinges, or sleeves without coats, or bows without violins; that is, unrelated to wholes or purposes which give them meaning.

The Seven Virtues

> *My child, obey me, choose virtue, and make my heart glad.*
> *Then I can say to those who taunt me,*
> *"The job well-done is the pupil well-taught."*
> PROVERBS 27:11

My Secret Meditation

_____

_____

_____

I'll Decide What's Right and What's Wrong

Nietzsche, who lost his faith, even in his atheism experienced God as a "robber behind the clouds," a kind of envious tyrant who tries to steal man's dearest possession, that is the affirmation of himself as the supreme decider of what is right and what is wrong.

For God and Country

People are fools to trust themselves.
The wise trust the Wisdom of God.
PROVERBS 28:26

My Secret Meditation

_____

_____

_____

A Final Exam

I f a box is filled with salt, it cannot be filled with sand, and if our hearts are filled with hatred of our neighbor, how can God fill them with His love?

We must forgive others, for on no other condition will our own sins be forgiven. It is as simple as that. There can be and there will be no mercy toward us unless we ourselves are merciful.

The real test of the Christian then is not how much he loves his friends, but how much he loves his enemies.

The Rainbow of Sorrow

When you try to please God,
He makes even your enemies to be at peace with you.
PROVERBS 16:7

My Secret Meditation

_____

_____

_____

17

The Secret of Power

When I stand up to talk, people listen to me; they will follow what I have to say. Is it any power of mine? Of course not. St. Paul says: "What have you that you have not received and you who have received, why do you glory as if you had not?"

But the secret of my power is that I have never in fifty-five years missed spending an hour in the presence of our Lord in the Blessed Sacrament. That's where the power comes from. That's where sermons are born. That's where every good thought is conceived.

Through the Year with Fulton Sheen

Do you want to be wise?
The first step is to trust and reverence the Lord!
PROVERBS 1:7

My Secret Meditation

_____

_____

_____

How to Get Rich

It is one of the paradoxes of Christianity that the only things that are really our own when we die are what we gave away in His name. What we leave in our wills is snatched from us by death; but what we give away is recorded by God to our eternal credit, for only our works follow us.

Footprints in a Darkened Forest

If you want to be rich, be generous to others!
If you hold on too tightly, you'll lose everything.
Yes, generous people shall be rich!
By watering others, they water themselves.
PROVERBS 11:24–25

My Secret Meditation

_____

_____

_____

Eye Banks and Blood Banks

Spiritual aid to needy souls has not kept pace with material aid for needy bodies. Since there are eye banks for the blind and blood banks for the anemic, why should there not be prayer banks for the fallen and self-denial banks for sinners?

Treasure in Clay

When you say, "We didn't know this,"
won't the Lord know you knew it?
Won't you be blamed for what you failed to do?
PROVERBS 24:12

My Secret Meditation

_____

_____

_____

A Prayer That Is Always Answered

I f anyone thinks that prayers are never answered, let him offer a prayer to the Lord that some suffering be sent to save a soul.

Bishop Sheen Writes

> *The Lord is far away from the wicked,*
> *but the righteous?*
> *He answers their prayers!*
> PROVERBS 15:29

My Secret Meditation

_____

_____

_____

A Wrong Way to Feel Right

We fit a creed to the way we live, rather than fitting the way we live to a creed. We suit religion to our actions, rather than actions to religion. We try to keep religion on a speculative basis in order to avoid moral reproaches on our conduct.

Bishop Sheen Writes

Stubborn fools always think they're right,
but if you're smart, you'll listen to advice.
PROVERBS 12:15

My Secret Meditation

_____

_____

_____

Are They Laughing at You?

True followers of Christ! Be prepared to have a world make jokes at your expense. You can hardly expect a world to be more reverent to you than to Our Lord. When it does make fun of your faith, its practices, abstinences, and rituals—then you are moving to a closer identity with Him Who gave us our faith.

Nor may you return sneer with sneer. We cannot fight God's battles with the weapons of Satan. Repaying jeer with jeer is not the response of a Christian, for under scorn Our Lord "answered nothing." The world gets more of its amusement from a Christian who fails to be Christian, but none from his respectful silence. Dogs bay at the moon all night, but the moon gives back no snarl. It goes on shining.

Characters of the Passion

Stubborn fools are quick-tempered;
if you're smart, you'll stay cool when insulted.
PROVERBS 12:16

My Secret Meditation

_____

_____

_____

 *23*

A Strange Silence

Why are pulpits which resound with the Name of Christ so silent about His Mother, who was chosen for such a dignity in the agelessness of eternity?

Treasure in Clay

Charm can be deceptive, and beauty soon fades,
but a woman who fears the Lord shall be praised.
PROVERBS 31:30

My Secret Meditation

_____

_____

_____

Whose Funeral Is It, Anyhow?

Imagine the funeral service of a person who had lived in sacramental and mystic union with Christ throughout his life. His body is dead beyond all doubt, but his soul lives, not only with natural immortality, which it possesses, but with the very life of God.

Suppose a pallbearer standing nearby is in the state of sin. In the eyes of God, it is the pallbearer who really is dead and if we were spiritually minded, we would weep over him and chant a requiem over his soul rather than the departed one. The real death is not the death of the body, but the death of the soul.

From the Angel's Blackboard

There is a wide open way that seems right to us,
but at the end of that road is death.
PROVERBS 16:25

My Secret Meditation

_____

_____

_____

25

Why Is There Pain?

There is a very great difference between pain and sacrifice: Pain is sacrifice without love. Sacrifice is pain with love. When we understand this, then we shall have an answer for those who feel that God should have let us sin without pain.

The Rainbow of Sorrow

Suffering cleanses us of sin.
PROVERBS 20:30

My Secret Meditation

_____

_____

_____

When Anger Isn't a Sin

Anger is no sin if the cause of anger is injustice to someone other than oneself.

Victory Over Vice

Speak out for those who can't speak for themselves;
plead for those who are doomed.
PROVERBS 31:8

My Secret Meditation

_____

_____

_____

I'm Going to Sue You!

Why is it that we can find excuses for our anger against our neighbor and yet we refuse to admit the same excuses when our neighbor is angry with us? We say others would forgive us if they understood us perfectly, and that the only reason they are angry with us is because "they do not understand."

Why is not that ignorance reversible? Can we not be as ignorant of their motives, as we say they are ignorant of ours? Does not our refusal to find an excuse for their hatred tacitly mean that under similar circumstances we ourselves will be unfit to be forgiven?

Victory Over Vice

Do not be in a hurry to sue anyone.
You might start something you can't finish
and make a fool of yourself.
If you have a complaint against your neighbors,
discuss the matter with them;
but if you discover a secret about them, keep it to yourself.
Otherwise, your gossip might cling to you!
PROVERBS 25:8–10

My Secret Meditation

_____

_____

_____

Why We Refuse to Forgive

Take any scene of action, let five people look upon it, and you get five different stories of what happened. No one of them sees all sides. Our Lord does and that is why He forgives.

But we know nothing about the inside of our neighbors' hearts—their motives, their good faith, the circumstances surrounding their actions—and hence we refuse to forgive.

Peace of Soul

Only the persons involved know their own bitterness or joy;
no one else can really share it.
PROVERBS 14:10

My Secret Meditation

Education and Character

Education once seemed the gateway to Heaven-on-earth for everyone. Now we have tried it, and we know that schooling alone will not save our society. Never before was there so much education, and never before so little arrival at the truth. The twentieth century is the century of the greatest attempt at universal education in the history of the world—and yet it is the century of the most terrible conflagrations, wars, and revolutions of history. We have stuffed our children's minds with facts, and neglected to teach them how to live.

Lift Up Your Heart

How foolish to pay tuition to educate
troublemakers who have no desire for Truth!
PROVERBS 17:16

My Secret Meditation

_____

_____

_____

God's Broken Adding Machine

If during life we forgive others from our hearts, on Judgment Day the all wise God will permit something very unusual to Himself: He will forget how to add. He will know only how to subtract. He Who has a memory from all eternity will no longer remember our sins. Thus we will be saved through Divine "Ignorance."

It may well be that if He looks on a hand that gives a kindly blessing to an enemy, He will forget that it was once a clenched fist red with the blood of Jesus Christ.

Victory Over Vice

Do not gloat when your enemies suffer.
Don't be happy when they fall;
for the Lord may take His hand off of them and lay it on you!
PROVERBS 24:17–18

My Secret Meditation

_____

_____

_____

31

Malicious Joy

Envy is sadness at another's good, and joy at another's evil. What rust is to iron, what moths are to wool, what termites are to wood, that is what envy is to the soul: the assassination of brotherly love.

Envy manifests itself in discord, hatred, malicious joy, backbiting, detraction, imputing of evil motives, jealousy, and calumny.

Victory Over Vice

Do not envy sinners.
You have a wonderful future ahead!
Trust the Lord and keep your eyes on Him.
He will never fail you.
Proverbs 23:17–18

My Secret Meditation

_____

_____

_____

Who Will Be in Heaven?

One day a woman said to Father John Vianney, the Curé of Ars in France, "My husband has not been to the sacraments or to Mass for years. He has been unfaithful, wicked, and unjust. He has just fallen from a bridge and was drowned—a double death of body and soul!"

The Curé answered: "Madam, there is a short distance between the bridge and the water, and it is that distance which forbids you to judge."

Treasure in Clay

Everyone enjoys giving good advice, and oh!
What a good feeling to say the right thing at the right time!
PROVERBS 15:23

My Secret Meditation

_____

_____

_____

＋═ 33 ═＋

I'm Okay? You're Okay?

We sit at the piano of life and insist that every note we strike is right—because we struck it.

We justify want of faith by saying, "I don't go to church, but I am better than those who do"; as one might say, "I don't pay taxes or serve the nation, but I am better than those who do."

If each man is his own judge and standard, then who shall say he is wrong?

Peace of Soul

We can always "prove" we're right,
but what does the Lord have to say?
PROVERBS 16:2

My Secret Meditation

_____

_____

_____

34

We Find What We Look For

Those who are charged with character formation will do well to lay hold of what is best in people. There is something good in everybody.

After the death of a street cleaner who had a reputation for dissolute living and infidelity and cruelty to his wife and children, most of his fellow street cleaners recalled all the evil about him—except one companion who said: "Well, whatever you say about him, there was one thing he always did well. He swept clean around the corners...." As we show mercy to others, God may show the Grace of His Mercy to us.

Lift Up Your Heart

If we search for good, we find God's favor;
if we search for evil, we find His curse.
PROVERBS 11:27

My Secret Meditation

_____

_____

_____

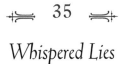

Whispered Lies

The chances are that there is a bit of jealousy, a bit of envy, behind every cutting remark and barbed whispering we hear about our neighbor. It is well to remember that there are always more sticks under the tree that has the most apples.

There should be some comfort for those who are unjustly attacked to remember that it is a physical impossibility for anyone to get ahead of us who stays behind to kick us.

Victory Over Vice

*The evil tongue slays three:
the slanderer, the slandered, and the listener.*
PROVERBS 18:21

My Secret Meditation

_____

_____

_____

Secret Shame and Heartache

To keep sin to oneself is worse than keeping a disease to oneself. A patient confides his physical or mental sickness to the doctor, as a student offers his ignorance to the teacher; why should not sin also have its confidante?

The memory of wrongdoing, if kept to oneself, will do one of two things: Either it will become a temptation to repeated sin, or its remorse will paralyze our moral efforts toward betterment with such despairing words as, "Oh, what's the use?"

What the hand is to the eye in providing relief from the speck, that the tongue ought to be to the heart in providing release from sin.

My tongue will tell the anger of my heart;

Or else my heart, concealing it, will break.

Peace of Soul

When we confess and forsake our sins,
God is faithful and just to show mercy.
PROVERBS 28:13

My Secret Meditation

_____

_____

_____

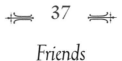

Friends

In every friendship hearts grow and entwine themselves together, so that the two hearts seem to make only one heart with only a common thought. That is why separation is so painful; it is not so much two hearts separating, but one heart being torn asunder.

Victory Over Vice

Some friends are friends in name only;
others are closer than sisters or brothers.
PROVERBS 18:24

My Secret Meditation

_____

_____

_____

The Really Rich Boy

The really rich boy need not wear good clothes to impress his friends with his wealth, but the poor boy may do so to create the false impression of wealth.

So it is with those who have nothing in their heads; they must be eternally creating the impression of how much they know, the books they have read, and the university from which they were graduated.

The saint never has to appear pious—but the hypocrite does.

Victory Over Vice

The good are guided by sincerity;
the hypocrite is destroyed by pretense.
Proverbs 11:3

My Secret Meditation

_____

_____

_____

Kitchen Sponges and Sore Thumbs

A sponge can absorb so much water and no more; a person's character can absorb so much praise and no more; the point of saturation is reached when the honor ceases to be a part of him and begins to stick out like a sore thumb.

The truly great are like St. Philip Neri who one day, seeing a criminal being led off to prison, said, "There goes Philip Neri, except for the grace of God."

Victory Over Vice

Pride brings disgrace;
modesty brings honor.
PROVERBS 29:23

My Secret Meditation

_____

_____

_____

God's Diet Plan

Gluttony is an inordinate indulgence in food or drink. It may manifest itself either in taking more than is necessary, or in taking it at the wrong time, or in taking it too luxuriously. It is sinful because reason demands that food and drink be taken for the necessities and conveniences of nature but not for pleasure alone.

Victory Over Vice

The good eat to live;
the wicked live to eat.
PROVERBS 13:25

My Secret Meditation

_____

_____

_____

A Five-Minute Health Routine

It is not particularly difficult to find thousands who will spend two or three hours a day in exercising, but if you ask them to bend their knees to God in five minutes of prayer, they protest that it is too long. Added to this is the shocking amount that is yearly spent not in the normal pleasure of drinking, but in its excess.

Victory Over Vice

Too much wine makes you rowdy,
hard liquor becomes your master.
You lose control and it makes a fool of you.
PROVERBS 20:1

My Secret Meditation

_____

_____

_____

42

Beauty Shops and Worms

When men begin to forget their souls, they begin to take great care of their bodies. If there is any indication of the present degeneration of society better than another, it is the excess of luxury in the modern world.

There are more athletic clubs in the modern world than there are spiritual retreat houses; and who shall count the millions spent in beauty shops to glorify faces that will one day be the prey of worms?

Victory Over Vice

Some are dead while still alive;
they vegetate because
they are blind to life's higher values.
PROVERBS 5:23

My Secret Meditation

_____

_____

_____

The Great Tragedy of Life

The great tragedy of life is not so much what men have suffered, but what they have missed. And what greater tragedy is there than to miss the peace of sin forgiven? There is no man living who, if he willed it, could not enjoy the spiritual food and drink which God serves to all who ask.

Calvary and the Mass

I call you, but you refuse to listen to me!
I stretch out my hands to you and you ignore me.
PROVERBS 1:24

My Secret Meditation

_____

_____

_____

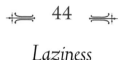 44

Laziness

Sloth is a malady of the will which causes us to neglect our duties. It may be either physical or spiritual.

It is physical sloth when it manifests itself in laziness, procrastination, idleness, softness, indifference, and nonchalance.

It is spiritual sloth when it shows itself in an indifference to character betterment, a distaste for the spiritual, a hurried crowding of devotions, a lukewarmness, and a failure to cultivate new virtue.

Victory Over Vice

Their own greedy desires destroy the lazy;
they lie around dreaming and refuse to work.
PROVERBS 21:25

My Secret Meditation

_____

_____

_____

Self-Centered and Miserable

Every self-centered person is a self-disrupted person. Nothing happens to him—he does something to himself.

Footprints in a Darkened Forest

Some people ruin themselves by their own foolishness,
and then they blame the Lord!
PROVERBS 19:3

My Secret Meditation

_____

_____

_____

My Candle Burns at Both Ends

Burning the candle at both ends for God's sake may be foolishness to the world, but it is a profitable Christian exercise—for so much better the light!

Only one thing in life matters: Being found worthy of the Light of the World in the hour of His visitation.

We need have no undue fear for our health if we work hard for the Kingdom of God; God will take care of our health if we take care of His cause. In any case, it is better to burn out than to rust out.

Victory Over Vice

You will live longer because of me;
I will add birthdays to your life!
PROVERBS 9:11

My Secret Meditation

_____

_____

_____

Shining Shoes for Jesus

If we could create worlds and drop them into space from our fingertips, we would please God no more than by dropping a coin into a tin cup. It is not what is done, but why it is done that matters. A bootblack shining a pair of shoes inspired by a Divine motive is doing more good for this world than all the conventions government can convene.

God Love You

It is sin to despise the poor,
but kindness brings blessings from God.
PROVERBS 14:21

My Secret Meditation

_____

_____

_____

When Our Lease Runs Out

When our lease on life runs out, there are two questions that will be asked:

1. The world will ask: "How much did he leave?"

2. The angels will ask: "How much did he bring with him?"

At death you will leave everything, but there is one thing you will not leave—your desire to live. You want the one thing the Cross brings you: Life through death.

Victory Over Vice

There are no pockets in shrouds:
your money won't help you on Judgment Day;
only righteousness will deliver you from death.
PROVERBS 11:4

My Secret Meditation

_____

_____

_____

How Old Do You Want to Be When You Die?

May we never die too soon! This does not mean not dying young. It means not dying with our appointed tasks undone.

It is indeed a curious fact that no one ever thinks of Our Lord as dying too young! That is because He finished His Father's business.

No matter how old we are when we die, we always feel there is something more to be done. Why do we feel that way, if it is not because we did not do well the tasks assigned to us?

Our task may not be great; it may be only to add one stone to the Temple of God. But whatever it is, do each tiny little act in union with your Savior who died on the Cross and you will *finish* your life. Then you will never die too young!

Victory Over Vice

Consult the Lord about your plans,
then whatever you do will prosper.
PROVERBS 16:3

My Secret Meditation

50

Nothing New Under the Sun

History bears witness to the fact that almost every radical economic revolutionist in the history of the world has been interested in only one thing—loot.

Peace of Soul

*A wicked politician is as dangerous to the poor
as a roaring lion or a ravenous bear.*
PROVERBS 28:15

My Secret Meditation

_____

_____

_____

How to Acquire a Heart of Gold

Man becomes like that which he loves. If he loves gold, he becomes like it—cold, hard, and yellow. The more he acquires, the more he suffers at surrendering even the least of it, just as it hurts to have a single hair pulled out even though your head is full of them.

Victory Over Vice

Wisdom is worth much more than gold,
and understanding should be chosen over silver.
PROVERBS 16:16

My Secret Meditation

_____

_____

_____

Two Secrets to Change Your Life

1. The more ties we have to earth, the harder will it be for us to die.
2. We were never meant to be perfectly satisfied here below.

Victory Over Vice

> *Two things in life are never satisfied:*
> *ambition and death.*
> PROVERBS 27:20

My Secret Meditation

_____

_____

_____

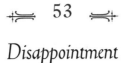

Disappointment

It is absolutely impossible for us to be perfectly happy here below. Nothing proves this more than disappointment. One might almost say the essence of life is disappointment. We look forward to a position, to marriage, to ownership, to power, to popularity, to wealth, and when we attain them we have to admit, if we are honest, that they never come up to our expectations. We are never thirsty at the borders of a well. Everything is disappointing except the Redemptive Love of our Lord.

Victory Over Vice

I love those who love me,
and if you seek me earnestly, you'll find me.
I have lasting riches, honor, and virtue for you.
My gifts are worth more than pure gold
and are superior to sterling silver.
PROVERBS 8:17–19

My Secret Meditation

_____

_____

_____

Is God All in the Mind?

Most contemporary psychiatrists have found flaws in Freud's philosophy of interpreting man in terms of sex rather than sex in terms of man. Is it not, therefore, time to point out another basic error of Freud, namely, making God a mental projection? How could the mind invent the idea of God as a father, unless God was already outside the human mind? Would anyone invent a fairy tale of a carriage changed into a pumpkin unless there was, in the real world, a pumpkin?

The divine spark in us did not result from an Oedipus complex; we were born with it. We can either respond to its gentle urging, or we can suppress it.

God Love You

Stop listening to teaching that contradicts
what you know to be true.
PROVERBS 19:27

My Secret Meditation

_____

_____

_____

Dirty Rivers and Bed-Hopping

We are living in the only period of the world's history which has denied human guilt and sin. All other generations saw a close relationship between sowing and reaping, between freedom and responsibility. Today, "Be cool" is the sophisticated way of saying "Do not be overly concerned with what is right because there is nothing that can be called wrong."

The only sins in our world are social sins, such as the cutting of taxes, and spoiling of rivers; but there is nothing wrong about bed-hopping and adultery. This makes sorrow for personal sins impossible.

God Love You

Winking at sin leads to tragedy;
bold reproof is kind.
Proverbs 10:10

My Secret Meditation

_____

_____

_____

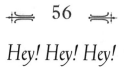

Hey! Hey! Hey!

Drifting is following the line of least resistance or, in psychological terms, being conformed to the moods and fashions of the time—being "with it"—whatever "it" means.

T.S. Eliot says that when everyone is running to a dangerous precipice, he who runs in the opposite direction is presumed to have lost his mind.

God Love You

Sometimes a way seems right,
but when it's too late to turn back, you find death.
PROVERBS 14:12

My Secret Meditation

_____

_____

_____

When You're Annoyed, Think of This!

It isn't hard to put up with others' foibles when we realize how much God has to put up with from us. There is a legend that one day Abraham was visited in the desert by an Arab who set up loud complaints of the food, the lodging, the bed, and the wine which his generous host had offered him. Finally Abraham became exasperated and was about to put him out. At that moment, God appeared and said: "Abraham, I have stood this man for forty years; can't you put up with him for one day?"

Through the Year with Fulton Sheen

Short-tempered people make mistakes,
and hate those who are patient.
PROVERBS 14:17

My Secret Meditation

_____

_____

_____

Feast or Fast

There are two basic philosophies of life. One is, first the feast and then the headache. The second is, first the fast and then the feast.

Bishop Sheen Writes

Those who are wise plan ahead,
but fools live for today.
PROVERBS 21:20

My Secret Meditation

_____

_____

_____

Religious Bad Men

The better we become, the less conscious we are of our goodness. If anyone admits to being a saint, he is close to being a devil. Jean Jacques Rousseau believed that of all men, he was the most perfect, but he had so many cracks in his soul that he abandoned his children after their birth.

The more saintly we become, the less conscious we are of being holy. A child is cute so long as he does not know that he is cute. As soon as he thinks he is, he turns into a brat. True goodness is unconscious.

Bishop Sheen Writes

Eating too much honey is not good;
neither is fishing for compliments.
PROVERBS 25:27

My Secret Meditation

_____

_____

_____

Golfing with Jack Nicklaus

The closer one gets to Christ, the less we think ourselves to be. Golfers may think themselves rather good until they play with Jack Nicklaus. When we see our lives in contrast to perfect innocence on a Cross, then we see how much we have failed.

God Love You

If you want to improve,
be willing to be corrected.
PROVERBS 10:17

My Secret Meditation

_____

_____

_____

61

Kindness on Death Row

One day Pope John XXIII went into a prison to visit the prisoners. He passed one cell and asked, "Who's in there?"

The warden said, "That's the death cell. The man in there killed his wife."

John spoke to him from outside the bars. He wouldn't answer. Pope John said to the warden, "Let me in."

The man faced the wall, would not turn around. John asked the warden, "What is he in here for?"

The warden repeated, "He killed his wife."

John said quietly, "Young man, I've never been married, but do you know that if I were married, I might have killed my wife, too?"

With that, the prisoner turned around, and embraced John.

God Love You

Do you try to be kind and good?
God notices and He will bless you.
PROVERBS 21:21

My Secret Meditation

_____

_____

_____

Winning Through Listening

Meditation is a more advanced spiritual act than saying prayers. It may be likened to the attitude of a child who breaks into the presence of a mother saying: "I'll not say a word, if you will just let me stay here and watch you!" Or, as a soldier once told the Curé of Ars: "I just stand here before the tabernacle; He looks at me and I look at Him."

Lift Up Your Heart

What a shame—yes, how stupid!—
to answer before you've listened!
PROVERBS 18:13

My Secret Meditation

_____

_____

_____

A Guaranteed Way to Change Behavior

If a person meditates consistently on God, a complete revolution takes place in that person's behavior.... Since Our Lord took the world's sins upon Himself, anyone who has dwelt on this truth will seek to take up the burdens of his or her neighbor, even though these burdens are not of our making—for the sins the Lord bore were not of His making, either. If our meditation stresses the merciful Savior Who forgave those who crucified Him, so we will forgive those who injure us, that we may be worthy of forgiveness. Such thoughts do not come from ourselves, for we are incapable of them; nor from the world, for they are unworldly thoughts. They come from God alone.

From the Angel's Blackboard

Have two goals: wisdom from God and common sense.
Don't let them slip away! They will bring you a gracious personality,
a fine reputation, God-fearing intelligence, and a long life.
PROVERBS 3:21-22

My Secret Meditation

_____

_____

_____

Look at Me!

The valet of the famed German Kaiser of World War I said: "I cannot deny that my master was vain. He had to be the central figure in everything. If he went to a christening, he wanted to be the baby; if he went to a wedding, he wanted to be the bride. If he went to a funeral, he wanted to be the corpse."

God Love You

First comes pride, then comes shame;
but the good and the wise are humble.
PROVERBS 11:2

My Secret Meditation

_____

_____

_____

How to Say I'm Sorry

Repentance is rather a dry-eyed affair. Tears flow in sorrow, but in repentance, sweat flows. It is not enough to tell God we are sorry and then forget all about it. If we broke a neighbor's window, we would not only apologize but also would go to the trouble of putting in a new pane. Since all sin disturbs the equilibrium and balance of justice and love, there must be a restoration involving toil and effort.

To see why this must be, suppose that every time a person did wrong he was told to drive a nail into the wall of his living room and that every time he was forgiven he was told to pull it out. The holes would still remain after the forgiveness. Thus every sin (whether actual or original) after being forgiven leaves "holes" or "wounds" in our human nature, and the filling up of these holes is done by penance; a thief who steals a watch can be forgiven for the theft, but only if he returns the watch.

Peace of Soul

*If you refuse to change, you will suddenly be crushed
and never have another chance.*

PROVERBS 29:1

My Secret Meditation

_____

_____

_____

The End of a Road

We are at the end of a tradition and a civilization which believes we could preserve Christianity without Christ: religion without a creed, meditation without sacrifice, family life without moral responsibility, sex without purity, and economics without ethics.

We have completed our experiment of living without God and have proven the fallacy of a system of education which calls itself progressive because it finds new excuses for sins.

The soul is gone, and what we call change is only decay.

The Seven Virtues

Where there is ignorance of God, crime runs rampant,
but peaceful the nation that knows and obeys His laws!
PROVERBS 29:18

My Secret Meditation

_____

_____

_____

When You're Lost and You Run Out of Gas

Analyzing your soul, you discover it to be like an auto that has run out of gas, and you are not quite sure of the right road. Hence you need someone not only to give you some fuel for your tank, but also someone to point out your destination.

If you have no religion at the present time, it may be because you rightly reacted against those bland assumptions that a few moral exhortations on Sunday will transform the world into the Kingdom of God.

You want a religion that starts not with how good you are, but with how confused you are.

From the Angel's Blackboard

> *The good seek advice from their friends;*
> *the wicked plunge ahead and sink.*
> PROVERBS 12:26

My Secret Meditation

_____

_____

_____

How to Know If You're a True Follower of Christ

True followers of Christ were meant to be at odds with the world:

- The pure of heart will be laughed at by Freudians.
- The meek will be scorned by the Marxists.
- The humble will be walked on by the go-getters.
- The liberal Sadducees will call them reactionaries.
- The reactionary Pharisees will call them liberals.

To all compromising Christians, a plea is made not to forget the word of our Savior: "He that shall deny me before men, I will also deny him before my Father who is in heaven."

The Seven Virtues

When the good compromise with the wicked,
they pollute a fountain and poison a spring.
PROVERBS 25:26

My Secret Meditation

_____

_____

_____

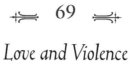

69

Love and Violence

Why do so many acts of rape end in murder of the victim?

As Tacitus said, it is "a characteristic of human nature to hate those whom we have injured."

The real test of pleasures is not as they come, but as they go. The victim of an evil desire becomes an object of bitter aversion, the violence which follows being a kind of expunging of guilt, not by striking one's own breast in repentance, but by striking the one who has been wronged.

God Love You

Good hates the badness of the bad.
Bad hates the goodness of the good.
PROVERBS 29:27

My Secret Meditation

_____

_____

_____

We Share a Common Burden

There is unfortunately a far greater unity among the enemies of God than among His friends. Hitler and Stalin buried their mutual hatred of each other because they found a greater hatred—God and religion.

Here is a common burden of all believers in God: relight the lamp of faith in the souls of men.

The Seven Virtues

The common bond of rebels is their guilt.
The common bond of believers is their virtue.
PROVERBS 14:9

My Secret Meditation

_____

_____

_____

Walk the Talk

If we followed the same rules for health that we do about religion, we would all be bedridden. It is not enough to talk about the necessity of health; we must do something practical about it—for example, eat, exercise, and rest.

So it is with religion. We must nourish ourselves with the truths of God, exercise our spiritual muscles in prayer, mortify ourselves of those things which are harmful to the soul, and be just as scrupulous in avoiding moral evil as we are in avoiding physical evil.

The Seven Virtues

My child,
always remember what I've taught you.
If you want a long and peaceful life,
follow my instructions!
PROVERBS 3:1–2

My Secret Meditation

_____

_____

_____

Building a New House

There is a story told of a woman who gave a fortune motivated by human glory, and occasionally a meager gift for a spiritual intention. When she went to heaven St. Peter showed her a tiny insignificant little house, dwarfed by all the mansions surrounding it.

"I cannot live in that," said the woman.

St. Peter answered: "Sorry, lady. That was the best I could do with the materials you sent me."

The Seven Virtues

When you help others in any way,
you are lending to the Lord—
and He pays high interest on your loan!
PROVERBS 19:17

My Secret Meditation

_____

_____

_____

The Saddest Words of All

A friendly meal given to an enemy in the name of Him Who loved us when we were His enemies, is worth more on the day of our judgment than a ten million dollar hospital given to perpetuate a family name.

There is no injustice in this. Each gets the reward we want. In one instance, the love of Christ; in the other, the memory of men. Of the latter, our Lord said the saddest words ever spoken: "They already have their reward."

The Seven Virtues

A generous person will be made rich.
What you give away comes back to stay.
PROVERBS 11:25

My Secret Meditation

_____

_____

_____

Fail-Proof Steps to Build Self-Esteem

Each day:

- Hold back the sarcastic word.
- Return a kindly answer to a sneer.
- Seal the lips on the scandal you just heard (which probably, like all scandals, is 99.99 percent untrue).

It is the motive that matters—do this out of love of God.

God Love You

Careless words stab like a sword.
Thoughtful words bring healing.
PROVERBS 12:18

My Secret Meditation

_____

_____

_____

Love Is a Choice

A ll love on this earth involves choice. When, for example, a young man expresses his love to a young woman and asks her to become his wife, he is not just making an affirmation of love; he is also negating his love for anyone else. In that one act by which he chooses her, he rejects all that is not her.

There is no other real way in which to prove we love a thing than by choosing it in preference to something else. Words and sighs of love may be, and often are, expressions of egotism or passion; but deeds are proofs of love.

We can prove we love our Lord only by choosing Him in preference to anything else.

The Seven Virtues

Above all else, control your emotions.
They influence everything in your life.
PROVERBS 4:23

My Secret Meditation

_____

_____

_____

Too Much Psychoanalysis

There is entirely too much psychoanalysis in the world; what is needed is a little more psychosynthesis. Hearts and minds have been analyzed to a point where they are nothing more than a chaotic mass of unrelated nerve impulses. There is need for Someone to pull them together, to give them a pattern of life and above all, peace.

The Seven Virtues

The whole universe, even Hell, is open to God's knowledge,
and so is every human heart!
He has all the solutions to all of our problems.

PROVERBS 15:11

My Secret Meditation

_____

_____

_____

Catholics, Jews, and Protestants

Protestants, Jews, and Catholics have God, morality, and religion in common. In the name of God, let us—Jews, Protestants, and Catholics—do two things:

1. Realize that an attack upon one is an attack upon all, since we are all one in God; it is not tolerance we need, but charity; not forbearance but love.

2. Begin doing something about religion, and the least we can do is say our prayers; to implore God's blessings upon the world and our country; to thank Him for His blessings; and to become illumined in the fullness of His truth. There is entirely too much talk about religion and not enough action.

The Seven Virtues

Even children can be known by the way they act—
whether what they do is pure and whether it is right.
PROVERBS 20:11

My Secret Meditation

_____

_____

_____

They've Got to Be Taught!

Freud has made a very keen observation about infancy, saying that a child only gradually learns to distinguish between himself and the outer world. What is known to be outside comes later.

He thinks everything is a gift which he gives himself!

When the child grows out of infancy, there are refusals of requests and even delays. The child now begins to make a distinction between himself and what is outside of himself. He is trained for maturity by being taught self-discipline, restraint, self-denial, consideration for others, and obedience. When this type of home training is given to the child, it grows up to be normal, with little egotism, but with a deep concern for others.

God Love You

Train your children in the way they should go,
and when they grow older, they will not depart from it.
PROVERBS 22:6

My Secret Meditation

_____

_____

_____

Things You Can't Take Back

Certain things that we have in us, once they are given out, are never meant to be taken back. One is the air we breathe. If we take that air back into ourselves, it poisons us. Love is another. When love is breathed out to another human heart, it is never meant to be taken back. If it is taken back, it suffocates and poisons us.

From the Angel's Blackboard

Hatred stirs old quarrels,
and makes mountains out of molehills,
but love is not easily offended.
PROVERBS 10:12

My Secret Meditation

_____

_____

_____

Death Is Always Important

Death is always important for it seals a destiny. Any dying man is a scene. Any dying scene is a sacred place. That is why the great literature of the past which has touched on the emotions surrounding death has never passed out of date.

But of all deaths in the record of man, none was more important than the death of Christ. Everyone else who was ever born into the world came into it to *live;* only our Lord came into it to *die.* Death was a stumbling block to the life of Socrates, but it was the crown to the life of Christ.

Calvary and the Mass

If you sin against Wisdom, you harm yourself.
If you hate Wisdom, you love death.
PROVERBS 8:36

My Secret Meditation

_____

_____

_____

Regrets, He Had a Few

Darwin tells us in his autobiography that in his love for the biological he lost all the taste which he once had for poetry and music, and he regretted the loss all the days of his life. Excessive love of the flesh kills the values of the spirit.

Victory Over Vice

If you despise God's word, you despise all authority,
and you will lose your capacity to listen and
your sense of discrimination;
but eager obedience to God will be rewarded.
PROVERBS 13:13

My Secret Meditation

_____

_____

_____

A Barrel of Apples

Every mortal has both an outer life and an inner life. The outer life is his reaction to environment, his wealth, his amusement, and his pleasures. His inner life is his character, his spirit, his motivation, and his heart.

Man is very much like a barrel of apples. The apples that are seen on the top are his reputation, but the apples down below represent his character.

How often the beauty of the inner life appears even amidst the decrepitude of a perishing body. Milton lost his sight, but his poetic vision increased.

Footprints in a Darkened Forest

The building of the young is aging toward destruction;
The destruction of the aged is building.
PROVERBS 16:31

My Secret Meditation

_____

_____

_____

Who Is Greedy?

Simply because a man has a great fortune, it does not follow that he is greedy. A child with a few pennies might possibly be more covetous. Material things are lawful and necessary in order to enable us to live according to our station in life, to mitigate suffering, to advance the Kingdom of God, and to save our souls. It is the pursuit of wealth as an end instead of a means to the above ends, which makes a man greedy. In this class of the greedy are the young woman who marries a divorced man for his money, the public official who accepts a bribe ... the capitalist who puts profits above human rights and needs, and the laborer who puts party power above the laborer's rights. Because a man has no money in his pockets is no proof he is not greedy; he may be poor with a passion for wealth far in excess of those who possess.

Lift Up Your Heart

Who is rich? Those who are thankful for what they have.
PROVERBS 10:22

My Secret Meditation

_____

_____

_____

Paying What We Owe

Our final epitaph will be written by God—not on monuments but on hearts. Those who received more talents from God will be more strictly judged. God has given me not only a vocation, but He enriched it with opportunities and gifts, which means that He will expect me to pay a high income tax on the Final Day.

Treasure in Clay

Don't fail to pay your debts on time.
Don't say, "I'll pay you tomorrow,"
if you can pay it today.
PROVERBS 3:27–28

My Secret Meditation

_____

_____

_____

Getting Even

Our Lord came to make reparation for the sin of anger, first by teaching us a prayer: "Forgive us our trespasses as we forgive those who trespass against us"; and then by giving us a precept: "Love your enemies, do good to them that hate you."

More concretely still, He added: "Whosoever will force thee one mile, go with him another two ... if a man take away thy coat, let go thy cloak also unto him."

For God and Country

If your enemies are hungry, feed them,
if thirsty, give them a drink.
This will make them feel ashamed,
and the Lord will reward you.
PROVERBS 25:21-22

My Secret Meditation

_____

_____

_____

Good Old Golden Rule Days

Modern man forged an educational system without discipline. He fashioned a philosophy which denied truth and made good and evil only relative to the individual. Then he labeled every attempt to restore authority as "Fascism."

For God and Country

When you submit to authority, you set a good example;
but when you spurn authority,
you cause others to go astray.
PROVERBS 10:17

My Secret Meditation

_____

_____

_____

Guilty as Sin?

There is no evidence whatever to sustain the position of some modern psychiatrists that consciousness of sin tends to make a person morbid.

To call someone an escapist because he or she asks God for forgiveness is like calling a householder whose home is on fire an escapist because he sends for the fire department. If there is anything morbid in the sinner's responsible admission of a violated relationship with divine love, this is a jovial sanity compared with the real and terrible morbidity that comes to those who are sick and who refuse to admit their illness.

Peace of Soul

You pay no attention to my counsel, and ignore my rebuke.
When trouble comes, then you will call upon me, but it will be too late.
You won't find me because you waited too long!
PROVERBS 1:25, 27, 28

My Secret Meditation

_____

_____

_____

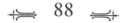

Are You a Critical Person?

M editation provides an artificial quiet by shutting out the din of day. It replaces the criticism of others, which is probably our mental habit, by a self-criticism which will make us less critical of others. The one who sees the most faults in his neighbor is the one who has never looked into his own soul. In meditation we discover that most of our neighbors are better than ourselves.

Lift Up Your Heart

With the mouth, a hypocrite destroys a neighbor,
but the godly understand human nature.
PROVERBS 11:9

My Secret Meditation

_____

_____

_____

You Will Be as Gods

In the modern world, pride disguises itself under the prettier names of *success* and *popularity*. A whole civilization has entered into a conspiracy to "make friends and influence people," by diplomatic self-deceit.

We are encouraged by quack psychologists to "trust ourselves" instead of trusting God. False confidence in the self is encouraged—although the only formula for a man's true contentment lies in his saying to God, "Thou alone art the Way, the Truth, and the Life!"

The modern man's desire to serve the best liquor, a woman's ambition to be the best dressed, the college sophomore's hope of being the most studiously unkempt, these are symptoms of an egotistical vanity which makes its owners dread not being noticed.

Lift Up Your Heart

The modest are promoted to honor;
the proud are promoted to shame.
PROVERBS 3:35

My Secret Meditation

How to Teach Children to Work Hard

Both my father and my mother were hard workers. Whenever we visited relatives, I could hear them say in the kitchen, "Ask Aunt Dee to leave the work to us," Dee being a nickname for my mother, Delia.

My father, whenever he would go to visit tenant farmers, would help build barns, reap the harvest, and do anything to keep himself busy.

Without it ever being expressed in so many words, I was brought up on the ethic of work.

Treasure in Clay

If you don't work, you don't eat.
PROVERBS 12:9

My Secret Meditation

_____

_____

_____

One Thing Jesus Didn't Show Us

When Jesus came to earth, He showed us everything lovely and beautiful in His character—except one thing. He showed us His power; He showed us His wisdom; He showed us His melting kindness; He showed us His sorrow; He showed us His tears; He showed us His forgiveness; He showed us His power over nature; He showed us His knowledge of human hearts.

But there was one thing He did not show; there was one thing He saved for those who do not take this world too seriously; there was one thing He saved for paradise; there was one thing He saved for those who, like poets and saints, have a divine sense of humor; there was one thing He saved for heaven that will make heaven heaven—and that was His smile!

From the Angel's Blackboard

A merry heart puts a smile on your face;
a sad face means your heart is breaking.
PROVERBS 15:13

My Secret Meditation

_____

_____

_____

Educated Goodness

Any system of education which fails to discipline the will also fails to train the character. Such teaching may succeed in making people into walking encyclopedias; it doesn't make them responsible citizens for a democracy. Education can never make a person better unless it teaches the true purpose of mankind—and the difficulties that must be overcome to realize that purpose.

Much education today is based on the Socratic error that ignorance of good is the cause of evil, and that all we need do to overcome evil is to give men information. If this were so, every educated man would be a good man; but we know this is not true.

Lift Up Your Heart

When the values of a nation crumble,
everything crumbles, including its government;
but with honest, wise, and godly leaders there is stability.
PROVERBS 28:2

My Secret Meditation

Angels Without Wings

God is generally operating behind secondary causes, like an anonymous benefactor. His direction of our lives is so hidden that most of us are unaware of how we were made an angel to help a neighbor, or how a neighbor was made an angel for us. They are everywhere—good angels—only we do not recognize them as such. The tragedy is that there are sometimes bad angels. They are evil persons who pull us down to vice. The world is a battlefield of angels.

From the Angel's Blackboard

Sometimes friendly words hide hatred in the heart.
PROVERBS 26:23

My Secret Meditation

_____

_____

_____

But You Said You Love Me!

Catastrophe can be to a world that has forgotten God what a sickness can be to a sinner; in the midst of it, millions might be brought not to a voluntary, but to an enforced crisis. A calamity would make vast numbers of people, who might otherwise lose their souls, turn to God.

Peace of Soul

Wounds from a friend are sweeter
than kisses from an enemy.
PROVERBS 27:6

My Secret Meditation

_____

_____

_____

In a Maximum-Security Prison

I once gave a retreat in a maximum security prison where there were nearly two thousand inmates. All of them thought, of course, that I was good and they were bad.

How could I begin? Well, I began by saying, "Gentlemen, I want you to know that there is one great difference between you and me. You got caught. I didn't."

In other words, we are all sinners.

Through the Year with Fulton Sheen

*When you are kind to others, you are kind to yourself;
when you demean others, you destroy yourself.*
PROVERBS 11:17

My Secret Meditation

_____

_____

_____

Sex Education

One of the great fallacies of some types of sex education is that it is assumed if children know some of the evils that result from excesses, they will avoid the reckless use of the libido. This is not true.

No mortal who sees a sign on a door marked "typhoid fever" has an urge to break down the door in order to contract the disease. But when the word "S E X" is written, there is a drive to break it down. The Spirit lusts against the flesh and the flesh lusts against the Spirit.

Peace of Soul

Listen to me, young people, and not only listen, but obey!
Take control of your emotions.
Don't let them control you!
PROVERBS 7:24, 25

My Secret Meditation

_____

_____

_____

Needed: A Statue of Responsibility

Socialism and the welfare state have a good origin and a bad origin. What is good about them is the recognition that we are brothers, live in a community, and are related as the parts of the body, each one needing his neighbor.

The bad origin of it is the growing sense of irresponsibility, the refusal to work, along with the denial that one should make a social contribution to society.

Footprints in a Darkened Forest

Hunger? It's good for us!
If we don't work, we don't eat!
PROVERBS 16:26

My Secret Meditation

_____

_____

_____

Stop the World, I Want to Get Off!

Suicide is like a chess player who cannot solve a problem before him, so he sweeps the pieces off the board. As this is no solution to the chess problem, a suicide is no solution to the problem of life. Animals do not commit suicide. It is only the eternal that can make a person despair. Despair is the absolute extreme of self-love. It turns its back on all others. In the end it is so disgusted with itself, it desires to be self-empty.

Through the Year with Fulton Sheen

What kind of person are you,
If you give up when trouble comes your way?
PROVERBS 24:10

My Secret Meditation

_____

_____

_____

The Past is History, the Future is Mystery

When a ship is sinking, we do not stop to analyze the chemistry of the water that pours into the holes. Pawing over our past blunders, like a rag picker, will never reveal to us the Pearl of Great Price; for that is to be found beyond ourselves.

No mind is creative of its own salvation, and other distracted minds cannot solve our distraction. Salvation will come by breaking the circle of our egotism, allowing the Grace of God to pour in.

Lift Up Your Heart

Certain people blame their parents for their troubles,
and consider themselves faultless for their sins.
PROVERBS 30:11–12

My Secret Meditation

_____

_____

_____

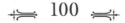

The Missing Link

During the last one hundred years scholars have been concerned about finding the human's relationship to the beast. Distressingly enough, during that same period of time humans have almost acted like beasts.

Christmas is the discovery of the Missing Link—not the link that binds us to the beasts, but the link that binds us to God.

Through the Year with Fulton Sheen

Who has gone up to heaven and come down?
Who has gathered the wind in His fists?
Who has carried water in His garment?
Who has set up the whole earth from one end to another?
What is His name or His son's name, if you know it?
Certainly, you must know!
PROVERBS **30**:4

My Secret Meditation

_____

_____

_____

The Movie of My Life

When the record of any human life is set down, there are three pairs of eyes who see it in a different light:

1. As I see it.
2. As others see it.
3. As God sees it.

Treasure in Clay

*The Lord sees everything we do;
the bad He punishes; the good, He rewards.*
PROVERBS 5:21

My Secret Meditation

_____

_____

_____

The Psychological Way/The Christian Way

The examination of the conscience never induces despair, always hope. Some psychologists, by the proper use of their method, have brought mental peace to individuals, but only because they have found a safety valve from mental pressure. They have let off steam, but they have not repaired the boiler. That is the business of the Church.

Peace of Soul

A counselor proposes; God disposes.
PROVERBS 19:21

My Secret Meditation

_____

_____

_____

The Right Way to Examine Your Conscience

In the examination of conscience a person concentrates less on his own sin than on the mercy of God—as the wounded concentrate less on their wounds than on the power of the physician who binds and heals the wounds.

As the empty pantry drives the housewife to the bakery, so the empty soul is driven to the Bread of Life.

Peace of Soul

Turn to me when I warn you.
Listen!
I will speak my mind
and explain my words to you.
PROVERBS 1:23

My Secret Meditation

_____

_____

_____

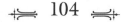

The Woman I Love

I think one of the major defects in world religions has been the absence of the feminine in Christian denominations where so little attention is paid to the Mother of Christ. It would be strange to visit a friend's home and yet never hear him speak of his mother.

Treasure in Clay

Vile and shameful children
crush their fathers
and chase away their mothers.
PROVERBS 19:26

My Secret Meditation

_____

_____

_____

They Will Say Two Things About You

At the end of a long life, one generally finds there are two things said: things too good to be true and things too bad to be true. When one enjoys some popularity in the world, such as the Lord has given to me in great measure, one is praised and respected even beyond desserts.

Treasure in Clay

If you want a good reputation with God and people,
then trust in the Lord with all your heart;
don't ever trust only yourself.
PROVERBS 3:4–5

My Secret Meditation

_____

_____

_____

Truth or Trash

When are you really most free? When you know the truth about something.

For example, you are free to draw a triangle on the condition that you give it three sides and not thirty-three.

You are free to draw a giraffe if you draw it with a long neck. If you do not accept the truth about the nature of giraffes and instead give your giraffe a short neck, you will find that you are not free to draw a giraffe.

You are free to drive your automobile in traffic on the condition that you obey traffic laws. You are free to pilot a plane if you respect the laws of gravitation and acknowledge the truth of aviation.

That is what Jesus meant when He said, "The Truth will make you free."

Through the Year with Fulton Sheen

The wise hunger for Truth;
fools feed on trash.
PROVERBS 15:14

My Secret Meditation

_____

_____

_____

Two Kinds of Hunger

The world to me suffers from two kinds of hunger. Our Western world, with its affluence, suffers from hunger of the spirit; the rest of the world from hunger of bread.

Take a circular map of the world, and run a finger around the thirtieth parallel, raising it slightly above China, and it will be discovered that most of the wealth, health, education, and scientific advancement is above the thirtieth parallel and much of the poverty and ignorance is below it. Christianity is above the thirtieth parallel; that is why it bears the burden of aiding the world's poor.

Footprints in a Darkened Forest

Give to the poor, your needs will be met;
close your eyes to the poor, your needs will grow.
PROVERBS 28:27

My Secret Meditation

_____

_____

_____

What Billy Ryan Told My Father

All the time we were in school my mother and my father sent the Sheen boys out to one of the two farms they owned by this time. The tenant farmer would accept us as hired hands on weekends and during the summer months.

In the early days during a lull in some heavy farm work, a jolly fat neighbor by the name of Billy Ryan said to my father, "Newt, that oldest boy of yours, Fulton, will never be worth a damn. He's always got his nose stuck in a book."

Treasure in Clay

Some people are paid for the work of their hands,
success comes to others through speaking ability.
PROVERBS 12:14

My Secret Meditation

_____

_____

_____

What Does JMJ Stand For?

In first grade, a suggestion was made by a good nun that we put at the top of every page the initials JMJ, standing for dedication to Jesus, Mary, and Joseph.

In the course of my life, I have written tens of thousands of pages. I do not believe I ever set my pen or pencil to paper without first having put that seal of dedication on my work.

All this makes me very certain that when I go before the Judgment Seat of Christ, He will say to me in His Mercy, "I heard my Mother speak of you."

Treasure in Clay

Many fine women have lived in the world,
but you are the finest of them all!
PROVERBS 31:29

My Secret Meditation

_____

_____

_____

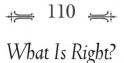

What Is Right?

There is an organ in my home. As I look at the keys on that organ, I could ask, "Which is good and which is bad? Which is right and which is wrong?" No one can say.

What makes a note right or wrong is its correspondence to a standard. A piece of music may be a standard. Once I have it before me, I know what I ought to do, what note I should hit, what note I ought not to hit. The piece of music is an absolute standard that tells me which note is right and which is wrong.

Like the organ, we also have a standard within us. It is our conscience. What is good and bad is in relationship to that unchanging standard *which is not of our own making.*

Through the Year with Fulton Sheen

Don't be conceited and proud;
it's safer to trust and reverence the Lord
than to trust and reverence yourself!
PROVERBS 3:7

My Secret Meditation

_____

_____

_____

When We Were a Couple of Kids

I have many fond memories of my schooling. In one of the very early grades, probably the first, I was kept after school because I had not learned to spell *which*. I tried spelling it a half-dozen or more ways, but to no avail. One little girl in back of me whispered w-h-i-c-h in my ear.

I met her again when she was eighty-three, and thanked her for furthering my education, *which* would have been much hampered without her whisper.

Treasure in Clay

Wisdom and kindness go together;
and speaking sweetly helps others learn.
PROVERBS 16:21

My Secret Meditation

_____

_____

_____

Who Decides What's Good?

A good is that which helps us in the attainment of purposes and goals and destinies *in accordance with an absolute standard.*

For instance, we do not draw our own maps, and decide what the distance from Chicago to New York will be. We do not arbitrarily set our own watches. We set them by a standard outside of us. When we buy material, we are not free to decide that a yard will be twenty-four inches instead of thirty-six inches.

Good is an absolute standard set not by ourselves, but by our Lord.

Through the Year with Fulton Sheen

Truth is the same in all generations;
lies last as long as the wink of an eye.
PROVERBS 12:19

My Secret Meditation

_____

_____

_____

Why Nietzsche Went Crazy

The teaching in modern universities is not as logical as Nietzsche who saw that man must either accept the Cross or go mad—and Nietzsche went mad.

For God and Country

What the wicked fear comes to them:
what the righteous long for comes to them.
PROVERBS 10:24

My Secret Meditation

_____

_____

_____

The Double-Cross

By denying the Cross of Christ, modern man did not escape a cross—no one can. Instead, he got a cross—the double-cross.

For God and Country

You refuse to listen to me;
You despise my every warning.
Now you will do things your way:
and be filled with your own corrupt schemes.
PROVERBS 1:30–31

My Secret Meditation

_____

_____

_____

The Wrong Kind of Anger

The wrong kind of anger is excessive, revengeful, and enduring. It is the kind of anger and hatred against God which has destroyed religion on one sixth of the earth's surface.

It is the anger which seeks to get even, to repay in kind, bump for bump, punch for punch, eye for eye, lie for lie; the anger of the clenched fist prepared to strike not in defense of that which is loved, but in offense against that which is hated; in a word, it is the kind of anger which will destroy our civilization unless we smother it by love.

Victory Over Vice

Do not say, "I'll get you for this!"
Wait for the Lord. He will save you.
PROVERBS 20:22

My Secret Meditation

_____

_____

_____

Picasso and God

When Picasso gives us part of a face, a twisted limb divided by a broken world, surmounted by a geometrical figure, we are staring at the tragedy of our times—a broken personality no longer resembling the Divine Image.

From the Angel's Blackboard

Courage can sustain a broken body,
but who can live with a broken spirit?
PROVERBS 18:14

My Secret Meditation

_____

_____

_____

Three Circles

M an may be thought of as three circles enclosing one another: a body, a mind or soul, and a spirit. The body puts us in touch with the world of senses, mountains, flowers, neon lights, perfume, songs of birds, and the touch of a hand. The mind (the soul) puts us in touch with science, reason, art, poetry, engineering, argumentation, how to make an atomic bomb, how to heal a wound, and the like. Briefly, it is self-consciousness. Finally, the spirit is not the Holy Spirit; it is that part of us which makes it possible to know God.

God Love You

Listen!
From God's mouth to our ears—absolute Truth.
PROVERBS 2:6

My Secret Meditation

_____

_____

_____

A Good Reason to Cry

I n the second beatitude—*Blessed are they who mourn, for they will be comforted*—it is not that mourners alone are blessed, but rather happy is the man who is sorry for the wrong things he has done, or as John Masefield put it, "the harm I've done being me."

Bishop Sheen Writes

The behavior of the wicked disgusts the Lord,
but He rewards those who try to be good.
PROVERBS 15:9

My Secret Meditation

_____

_____

_____

The Unforgivable Sin

The worst thing in the world is not sin; it is the denial of sin by a false conscience—for that attitude makes forgiveness impossible. The unforgivable sin is the denial of sin.

But until that sorry stage is reached, despite the failure of false starts, the short breathing spells between relapses, so long as there is real remorse, the voice of God is still being heard, and no case is hopeless. Such a soul may already be dead to Divine Love; but in its moments of turmoil, it is not dead to Divine Fear, and that can stir it into conscious life again.

It is often said that people have their hell here and now; they do have hell in this life, but not the whole of it. Hell and Heaven both begin for us on earth.

God Love You

Everything is in the hands of Heaven,
except the fear of Heaven.
PROVERBS 1:29

My Secret Meditation

_____

_____

_____

Three Surprises in Heaven

How God will judge my life I know not, but I trust He will see me with mercy and compassion. I am only certain there will be three surprises in Heaven. First of all, I will see some people whom I never expected to see. Second, there will be a number whom I expect who will not be there. And—even relying on God's mercy— the biggest surprise of all may be that I will be there.

Treasure in Clay

Do you trust Me?
Then you shall live in peace and safety, unafraid.
PROVERBS 1:33

My Secret Meditation

_____

_____

_____

Afterword

The Ancient and Powerful Art of Christian Meditation

The notion of Christian meditation confuses some people. That's understandable. During the sixties, four fabulous young rock-and-roll superstars made headlines around the world when they slung their guitars across their backs and traveled to India to pay homage to a man with a long white beard who wore robes and carried a flower. The Beatles came back extolling the ecstasy and life-changing intensity of meditation. Hundreds of thousands thronged to sample the mysteries of an apparently simple and powerful new activity.

Television talk shows rushed to feature movie stars, politicians, and other notables who claimed Hindu and Buddhist meditation techniques were giving them incredible inner peace and health. Almost overnight, it seemed, words like *Transcendental Meditation* (TM), *yoga, guru,* and *mantra* had entered our nation's lexicon.

As the cultural phenomenon mushroomed, meditation attracted the attention of serious researchers. Using scientific methods, they discovered an intriguing fact: Whether based on Hindu or Buddhist techniques, meditation of any kind produces salient results. Blood pressures fall. Heart rates slow.

These scientific disclosures gave Eastern meditation new respectability—and a deeper hold on the hearts and minds of millions. Inevitably, meditation mania slipped into many of America's churches, temples, and public schools. Adherents promoted it as the answer to mental, physical, or behavioral problems in young and old.

Meanwhile, concerned Christian scholars, including Fulton J. Sheen, warned that, however laudable the results of yoga and TM, without Christ the meditation techniques are powerless to touch the fundamental discord at the root of human unhappiness.

That was the golden thread woven throughout Fulton J. Sheen's entire life: *the peace of God that everyone seeks is available to all through His Son, Jesus Christ our Lord.*

The Bible and Meditation

From Genesis to Revelation, the practice of meditation is both explicit and implicit. The first explicit mention is in Genesis 24:63. Isaac, following the death of his beloved mother, turned to a practice that apparently was as natural a way to handle grief in the days of antiquity as it is today: "And Isaac went out to meditate in the field at the eventide: and he lifted up his eyes, and saw, and, behold, the camels were coming." Riding on one of those camels was the young woman who was to become Isaac's wife, the beautiful Rebekah.

In the Psalms, you'll find more than a dozen truly magnificent references to meditation as a familiar way to actually experience the supernatural presence of God.

And who can forget the poignant figure of Jesus just before He began His earthly ministry? All alone, He walked into the desert to meditate with His Father.

Fulton J. Sheen's Three Steps to Meditation

According to Fulton Sheen, three powers of the soul are used in Christian meditation: the memory, the intellect, and the will. By memory we recall His goodness and our blessings. With the intellect, we recall what is known of His life, truth, and love. With the will, we strive to love Him above all else.

"It is a little like a daydream or a reverie," Bishop Sheen wrote. "Instead of using the imagination to build castles in Spain, we use the will to make resolutions that will draw us nearer to one of the Father's mansions."

Anyone can learn to meditate by following steps taken by the disciples in the gospel account of the first Easter Sunday. On that day in their sadness they fell into talking about Our Lord with a traveler they had met by chance on the Emmaus Road.

First, they spoke about Jesus, not realizing He was present. So our first step is to forget about ourselves, to simply talk to God about Jesus. Talk openly to Him about His Son—His grace, His life, His death, His tenderness, His patience, His birth, His childhood, His tears.

Sometimes the mind tends to wander wildly and persistently with thoughts of our own plans and problems, our own death, our own tenderness or lack of it, our own patience or impatience, our own birth, our own childhood, and our own tears. When that happens, with an act of the will, bring the mind back to Jesus.

At first, it may seem impossible. Simply whisper His Name over and over and over. If your entire meditation is nothing more than breathing His Name a thousand times, the sound will still echo throughout the universe to heaven itself. *Jesus, Jesus, Jesus.*

The next step is *listening:* When Our Lord disclosed His presence to the disciples, unfolding to them the meaning of His Passion and Death, *they listened.* After we have talked to God about His Son, our self-absorption will be replaced with humble listening.

Finally, to the disciples came *communion,* shown in the gospel as the breaking of bread. Fulton Sheen describes this final step in meditation as "a spiritual communion, a moment so sweet, we will reluctantly abandon it, even when the day is far spent and fatigue is great."

Practical Effects of Christian Meditation

Christian meditation improves our behavior. Nothing ever happens in the world that does not first happen inside a mind. Said Fulton Sheen, "Our thoughts make our desires, and our desires are the sculptors of our days."

Christian meditation cures us of the habit of self-deception. The silence that meditation demands is the best cure for this; in silence the workmen of the soul clear away the rubbish, as trash collectors clean our cities in the quiet night.

Christian meditation gives us contact with new sources of power and energy. There is a moment in every good meditation when the God-life enters our life, and another moment when our life enters the God-life. These events transform us utterly. Sick, nervous, fearful people are made well by this communion of creature with Creator, this letting God into the soul.

A distinguished psychiatrist, J.D. Hadfield, has said: "I attempted to cure a nervous patient with suggestions of quiet and confidence, but without success, until one day I linked these suggestions to that faith in the power of God which is the substance of the Christian's confidence and hope. Then the patient became strong!"

Do you want to be strong? Do you want confidence and inner peace? Do you want to make the best of your life?

Fulton Sheen has shown us a way that cannot fail—but no one can do it for you. It begins with an act of the will: Walk into the desert. Go as Jesus did. Bend your knees and whisper His Name. Then listen!

Parts of Fulton J. Sheen's "Three Steps in Christian Meditation" and "Practical Effects of Christian Meditation" were condensed and paraphrased from Fulton J. Sheen's *Lift Up Your Heart.*

Sources Quoted or Consulted

Sources by Fulton J. Sheen:

"Bishop Sheen Writes," (a series of columns that appeared in national newspapers in the 1950s-1970s).

Calvary and the Mass. New York: P.J. Kenedy & Sons, 1936.

Characters of the Passion. New York: P.J. Kenedy & Sons, 1947.

For God and Country. New York: P.J. Kenedy & Sons, 1941.

From the Angel's Blackboard. Liguori, Mo.: Triumph, 1995.

Footprints in a Darkened Forest. New York: Meredith, 1967.

"God Love You" (a series of articles that appeared from the 1950s-1970s in Catholic newspapers).

Lift Up Your Heart. New York: McGraw-Hill, 1950.

Peace of Soul. New York: McGraw-Hill, 1949; Liguori, Mo.: Triumph, 1997.

The Rainbow of Sorrow. New York: P.J. Kenedy & Sons, 1938.

The Seven Virtues. New York: P.J. Kenedy & Sons, 1940.

Through the Year with Fulton Sheen. Ann Arbor, Mich.: Servant, 1985.

Treasure in Clay. Garden City, N.Y.: Doubleday/Image, 1982; San Francisco: Ignatius, 1993.

Victory Over Vice. New York: P.J. Kenedy & Sons, 1939.

Other sources:

The Book. (Wheaton, Ill.: Tyndale House, 1979).

Cohen, Rev. Dr. Abe. *Proverbs Hebrew Text & English Translation.* London: Soncino, 1952.

God's Word. Grand Rapids, Mich.: World Publishing, 1995.

The New American Bible for Catholics. Iowa Falls, Ia.: World Bible Publishers, 1991.

Plaut, W. Gunther. *The Book of Proverbs.* New York: Union of American Hebrew Congregations, 1961.